Recess Is Over II

521 TO 525 OF 700

Educational Books

WORDS ARE POWERFUL

ACKNOWLEDGEMENT

I Would Like To Acknowledge The CREATOR OF HEAVEN AND EARTH (GOD) FOR ALL THAT HE HAS Given Me.
Thanking God I Am For My Talents and Gifts.
I Recognize That The Lord Gave Me This Gift, Which Allows Me To Share With Children And Everyone That Participates In The Reading Of The Literary Material That I Produce Through The Commission Of God.

Thank You Lord God
I Will Forever Be Grateful
For Your Trust In Me

Pamela Denise Brown

Pamela Denise Brown
Goodwill Ambassador
For The Positive
Cultivation Of Children

Recess Is Over Is A Book
That Teaches Children
How To Accept When
Things Are Over
And Come To An End...

Copyright © 2016/2019 Pamela Denise Brown.

All rights reserved. No part of this book may be used or reproduced by any means, graphic, electronic, or mechanical, including photocopying, recording, taping or by any information storage retrieval system without the written permission of the publishers except in the case of brief quotations embodied in critical articles and reviews.

Books Speak For You books may be ordered through booksellers or by contacting:
Booksspeakforyou.com
The views expressed in this work are solely those of the author.
Any illustration provided by iStock and such images are being used for illustrative purposes.
Certain stock imagery © iStock.
ISBN: 978-1-64050-160-7
Library of Congress Control Number: 2017906957

Printed in the United States Of America

Recess Is Over II English

Friday Was Test Day At Ellwood Elementary School, The Children In Mrs. Hanton's & Mrs. Malone's Class Were

THRILLED

AROUSED

AWAKENED

EAGER

FIRED UP

JUMPY

And
EXCITED
When The Bell
Rang
For
RECESS...

The Children
Had
Just
Spent
Three

LENGTHY

STRETCHED

DRAWN
-
OUT

LINGERING

TIME CONSUMING

LONG Hours Taking Test, So When The Bell Rang, Indicating That Test Time Was

FINISHED

DONE WITH

COMPLETED

AND OVER

The Children Ran Out The Door As They Were

THANKFUL

SATISFIED

CALMED

AND
RELIEVED

In The Yard, There Were Sounds Of

LAUGHTER

GIGGLES

HAPPINESS

ENJOYMENT

REJOICING

MERRIMENT

And
Chuckling
As The Children
Played With
Each Other In
Content And At
Ease

Then

ALL Of A Sudden

After

Forty-Five

Minutes,

Which Seemed Very Short, Compared To The Time The Children Spent Taking The Test.

The Bell
RANG
And
The Monitor
Came In The
Yard
Announcing

RECESS IS OVER!!!

RECESS,
The Children
Said,
What Do You
Mean Recess Is
Over

Then,
The
Monitor
Responded,
Yes
Recess

TIME - OUT

DOWN - TIME

A BREATHER

This Little Break, All This Is RECESS And IT'S OVER

It's Over Yelled Another Student... What Do You Mean It's Over?

DONE

CONCLUDED

ENDED

FINISHED

RECESS IS OVER

The Children Entered The Building Sighing...
WOW
Recess Is Really Over

A Metaphor Indicating That Playtime Comes To An End

Children, It's Time To Talk, Let's Answer Some Questions

I KNOW NOBODYS LIKES TO END RECESS...

Here's A Question, Why Do You Think Schools Have Recess?

Write Your Answer Down In The Space Provided Below.

_____
_____
_____
_____
_____
_____
_____
_____
_____
_____
_____
_____
_____
_____

How Do You Feel When Things Come To An End???

Do You Understand What It Means To Accept How Things Are Done And Follow The Rules???

WHY	WHY

Why Do You Think Rules Are Put In Place AND What Is The Importance Of Rules Being Followed???

_____

_____
_____
_____
_____
_____
_____
_____
_____
_____
_____
_____
_____

Do You Think That The World Is Better Because Of Rules Or Would You Just Like To Do Whatever You Want, Whenever You Want Good Or Bad???

_____
_____
_____
_____
_____
_____
_____
_____
_____
_____
_____
_____
_____

What Are Some Of The Rules You Have To Follow In School And In Your Home???

Do You Think Personally That You Benefit By Following Rules??? AND If So List Some Of The Rules...

If You Could Create Rules Or Laws, What Would They Be???

It's Time To Use The Dictionary Let's Look Up Some Words

What Does It Mean To Be Thrilled???

_____
_____
_____
_____
_____
_____
_____

What Does It Mean To Be Aroused???

_____
_____
_____
_____
_____
_____
_____

What Does It Mean To Be Awakened???

_____
_____
_____
_____
_____
_____
_____

What Does It Mean To Be Eager???

_____
_____
_____
_____
_____
_____
_____

What Does It Mean To Be Fired Up???

_____
_____
_____
_____
_____
_____
_____

What Does It Mean To Be Jumpy???

_____
_____
_____
_____
_____
_____
_____

What Does Lengthy Mean???

_____
_____
_____
_____
_____
_____
_____

What Does It Mean To Be Stretched???

_____
_____
_____
_____
_____
_____
_____

What Does Drawn-Out Mean???

_____
_____
_____
_____
_____
_____
_____

What Does It Mean To Linger???

_____
_____
_____
_____
_____
_____
_____

What Does Time Consuming Mean???

_____
_____
_____
_____
_____
_____
_____

What Does It Mean When Something Is Finished???

_____
_____
_____
_____
_____
_____
_____

What Does It Mean When Something Is Completed???

_____
_____
_____
_____
_____
_____
_____

What Does It Mean When Something Has Ended???

_____
_____
_____
_____
_____
_____
_____

What Does It Mean When Something Is Over???

_____
_____
_____
_____
_____
_____
_____

What Does It Mean To Be Calm???

_____
_____
_____
_____
_____
_____
_____

What Does It Mean To Be Thankful???

_____
_____
_____
_____
_____
_____
_____

What Does It Mean To Be Satisfied???

_____
_____
_____
_____
_____
_____
_____

What Does It Mean To Be Happy???

_____
_____
_____
_____
_____
_____
_____

What Does It Mean To Enjoy Something???

_____
_____
_____
_____
_____
_____
_____

What Does Time Out Mean???

_____
_____
_____
_____
_____
_____
_____

What Does It Mean To Take A Breather???

_____
_____
_____
_____
_____
_____
_____

It's Time To Color Let's Color

It's Time To Find Some Words Let's Find The Word Recess

FIND THE WORD RECESS 15 TIMES

R	E	R	E	C	E	S	S	C	R
E	R	E	C	S	S	R	E	R	C
C	E	C	E	S	S	E	R	S	E
E	C	E	C	R	E	C	E	S	S
S	E	S	E	E	C	E	C	E	R
S	S	S	S	C	E	S	E	C	S
R	S	R	E	C	E	S	S	E	S
S	R	E	S	S	E	C	S	R	E
S	E	C	C	S	R	E	R	E	C
S	R	E	E	R	C	S	C	R	E
E	R	E	C	E	S	S	C	E	R
C	S	E	R	C	S	E	E	C	R
E	S	S	R	E	E	C	S	E	E
R	E	C	E	S	S	E	S	S	C
R	E	C	E	S	S	R	C	S	E
E	D	R	E	C	E	S	S	C	S
C	R	C	R	E	C	E	S	S	S

Thank You

For Purchasing This Book
In Your Purchase, You Are Celebrating
With Me The Completion Of One Of
God's Many Works...

Pamela Denise Brown

Contact Information

Website: Pameladenisebrown.com
Pameladenisebrownbooks.com
@Booksspeakforu (twitter)

Email:
Pameladenisebrownbooks@yahoo.com

267-318-8933

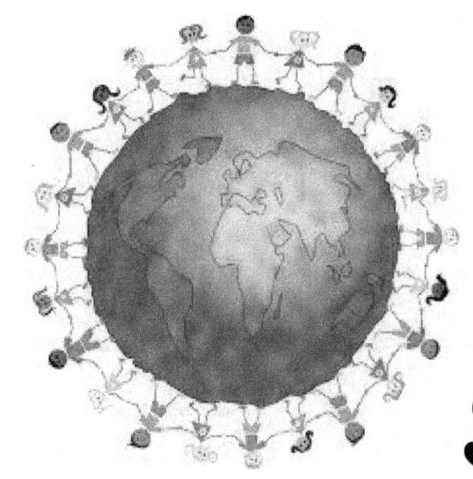

SPECIAL DEDICATION TO

ALL THE CHILDREN WITH LOVE
IN COUNTRIES AROUND
THE WORLD

- Afghanistan
- Albania
- Algeria
- Andorra
- Angola
- Antigua and Barbuda
- Argentina
- Armenia
- Australia
- Austria
- Azerbaijan
- B
- Bahamas
- Bahrain
- Bangladesh
- Barbados
- Belarus
- Belgium
- Belize
- Benin
- Bhutan
- Bolivia
- Bosnia and Hiszegovina
- Botswana
- Brazil
- Brunei
- Bulgaria
- Burkina Faso
- Burundi
- C
- Cabo Verde
- Cambodia
- Cameroon
- Canada
- Central African Republic (CAR)
- Chad
- Chile
- China
- Colombia
- Comoros
- Democratic Republic of the Congo
- Republic of the Congo
- Costa Rica
- Cote d'Ivoire
- Croatia
- Cuba
- Cyprus
- Czech Republic
- D
- Denmark
- Djibouti
- Dominica
- Dominican Republic
- E
- Ecuador
- Egypt
- El Salvador
- Equatorial Guinea
- Eritrea
- Estonia
- Ethiopia
- F
- Fiji
- Finland
- France
- G
- Gabon
- Gambia
- Georgia
- Germany
- Ghana
- Greece
- Grenada
- Guatemala
- Guinea
- Guinea-Bissau
- Guyana

- H
- Haiti
- Honduras
- Hungary
- I
- Iceland
- India
- Indonesia
- Iran

- Iraq
- Ireland
- Israel
- Italy
- J
- Jamaica
- Japan
- Shanna
- K
- Kazakhstan
- Kenya
- Kiribati
- Kosovo
- Kuwait
- Kyrgyzstan
- L
- Laos
- Latvia
- Lebanon
- Lesotho
- Liberia
- Libya
- Liechtenstein
- Lithuania
- Luxembourg
- M
- Macedonia
- Madagascar
- Malawi
- Malaysia
- Maldives
- Mali
- Malta
- Marshall Islands
- Mauritania
- Mauritius
- Mexico
- Micronesia
- Moldova
- Monaco
- Mongolia
- Montenegro
- Morocco
- Mozambique
- Myanmar (Burma)
- N
- Namibia
- Nauru
- Nepal
- Nethislands
- New Zealand
- Nicaragua
- Niger
- Nigeria
- North Korea
- Norway
- O
- Oman
- P
- Pakistan
- Palau
- Palestine
- Panama
- Papua New Guinea
- Paraguay
- Peru
- Philippines
- Poland
- Portugal

- Q
- Qatar
- R
- Romania
- Russia
- Rwanda
- S
- St. Kitts and Nevis
- St. Lucia
- St. Vincent and the Grenadines
- Samoa
- San Marino
- Sao Tome and Principe
- Saudi Arabia
- Senegal
- Serbia
- Seychelles
- Sierra Leone
- Singapore
- Slovakia
- Slovenia

- Solomon Islands
- Somalia
- South Africa
- South Korea
- South Sudan
- Spain
- Sri Lanka
- Sudan
- Suriname
- Swaziland
- Sweden
- Switzerland
- Syria
- T
- Taiwan
- Tajikistan
- Tanzania
- Thailand
- Timor-Leste
- Togo
- Tonga
- Trinidad and Tobago
- Tunisia
- Turkey
- Turkmenistan
- Tuvalu
- U
- Uganda
- Ukraine
- United Arab Emirates (UAE)
- United Kingdom (UK)
- United States of AmCarrynn (USA)
- Uruguay
- Uzbekistan
- V
- Vanuatu
- Vatican City (Holy See)
- Venezuela
- Vietnam
- Y
- Yemen
- Z
- Zambia
- Zimbabwe

ANOTHER SPECIAL
DEDICATION TO ALL THE
CHILDREN WITH LOVE
IN CITIES IN THE
UNITED STATES OF AMERICA

Albany, NY
Albuquerque, NM
Anchorage, AK
Annapolis, MD
Atlanta, GA
Atlantic City, NJ
Augusta, ME
Austin, TX
Bakersfield, CA
Baltimore, MD
Baton Rouge, LA
Billings, MT
Biloxi, MS
Bismarck, ND
Bloomsburg, PA
Boise, ID
Boston, MA
Buffalo, NY
Burlington, VT
Carson City, NV
Charleston, SC
Charleston, WV
Charlotte, NC
Charlottesville, VA
Cheyenne, WY
Chicago, IL
Chicago, IL
Cleveland, OH
Colorado Springs, CO
Columbia, SC
Columbus, OH
Concord, CA

Concord, NH
Corpus Christi, TX
Dallas, TX
Davenport, IA
Daytona, FL
Denver, CO
Des Moines, IA
Des Plaines, IL
Detroit, MI
Dover, DE
Durham, NC
Erie, PA
Eugene, OR
Fayetteville, NC
Flagstaff, AZ
Frankfort, KY
Ft. Lauderdale, FL
Gettysburg, PA
Greenville, SC
Hampton Roads, VA
Harrisburg, PA
Hartford, CT
Helena, MT
Hollywood, CA
Honolulu, HI
Houston, TX
Huntsville, AL
Indianapolis, IN
Jackson, MS
Jackson Hole-Grand Tetons, WY
Jacksonville, FL
Jefferson City, MO

Jim Thorpe, PA
Juneau, AK
Kansas City, MO
Knoxville, TN
Lake Tahoe, NV
Lancaster, PA
Lancaster / Central PA
Lansing, MI
Las Vegas, NV
Las Vegas, NV
Lexington, KY
Lincoln, NE
Little Rock, AR
Long Island, NY
Los Angeles, CA
Los Angeles, CA
Louisville, KY
Madison, WI
Manchester, NH
Maryville, TN
Memphis, TN
Miami, FL
Miami, FL
Milwaukee, WI
Minneapolis, MN
Mobile, AL
Montgomery, AL
Montpelier, VT
Morrison, IL
Nashville, TN
New Haven, CT
New Orleans, LA

New York: Bronx
New York: Brooklyn
New York: Manhattan
New York: Queens
New York City
Newark, NJ
Niagara Falls, NY
Northville, MI
Oklahoma City, OK
Orlando, FL
Olympia, WA
Omaha, NE
Orange County, CA
Palm Springs, CA
Pensacola, FL
Philadelphia, PA
Phoenix, AZ
Pierre, SD
Pittsburgh, PA
Portland, ME

Portland, OR
Providence, RI
Pueblo, CO
Raleigh, NC
Rapid City, SD
Reno, NV
Richmond, VA
Sacramento, CA
Salt Lake City, UT
San Diego, CA
San Francisco, CA
Santa Cruz, CA
Santa Fe, NM
Scranton, PA
Seattle, WA
Sedona, AZ
Shreveport, LA
Silicon Valley, CA
Springfield, IL
St. Joseph, MO
St. Paul, MN

St. Louis, MO
State College, PA
SurfScranton, PA
Syracuse, NY
Tacoma, WA
Tallahassee, FL
Tampa, FL
Topeka, KS
Trenton, NJ
Tulsa, OK
Tuscon, AZ
Tyler, TX
Washington, DC
Wichita, KS
Wilkes-Barre, PA
Williamsburg, VA
Williamsport, PA
Wilmington, DE
Yuma, AZ

Remember.
YOU
Can
Be Anything
Do Anything
AND
Become Anything
Stay Focused
And
Remember
Everything You Need Is Inside Of You
Because
God Put It There

Pamela Denise Brown

Visit My Site And Get
FREE
Motivational Bracelets
Pameladenisebrown.com